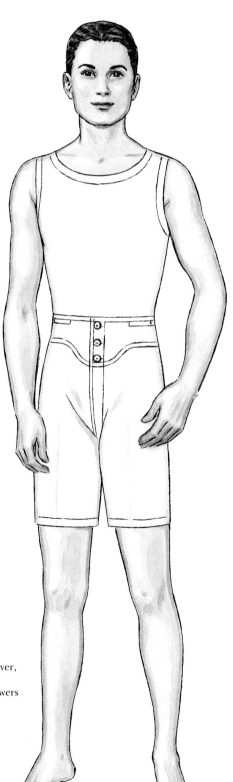

Marianne Brown, narrator
Vest and bloomers of flesh-colored rayon

James Reid, Indian Detours driver,
Grand Canyon
Cotton knit undershirt and drawers

Grandmother Brown, Marianne's grandmother, Waynoka, Oklahoma
Camisole and underskirt of silk crepe de chine

The Journal of Marianne Brown

Waynoka, Oklahoma

June 7, 1922: Grandmother Brown is always telling me that my life will be a piece of history one day. I'm not so sure anyone reading about the history of Woods County, Oklahoma, will want to know about a seventeen-year-old girl's life. Nothing unusual ever happens here. But I love Gramma's diaries that tell about my grandparent's homestead on the Cherokee Strip in the 1890s, so maybe my granddaughter will want to read about my life on father's farm along the Cimarron River?

June 10, 1922: Today Gramma and I went into town, as we do every Saturday, and after Gramma finished her errands we stood on the Waynoka railroad platform and awaited the arrival of the supper train, westbound from Kansas City. There are always many Waynokans standing around the platform before the train comes in, talking and laughing, sharing stories and gossip. When the Santa Fe comes roaring in, the Harvey House bus boy begins pounding on a gong, and inside the dining room, you should see those Harvey Girls hustle and bustle! The disembarking passengers walk across the hot platform, blinking under the bright summer sun. Sometimes they nod and say hello; at other times they just walk right by, dressed in their fine clothes. They must be shocked to see our little town: hardly any trees, and when the wind blows, there is more sand than air to breathe! I ask Gramma where she thinks the passengers have come from, where they live, and what they have seen, traveling the Santa Fe trains across the country.

June 15, 1922: Father will be in Waynoka all day today. He is meeting several salesmen coming in on the train from Kansas and will carry them and their goods to the local merchants in his dray. Sometimes I go along with him, but today Gramma and I are sewing. We have sewn dresses together since mother died of influenza five years ago. At first we sewed because we were sad, and it helped to talk about mother, and how we missed her, while we worked. We still miss her, but now we sew together because we enjoy spending time together on the cool porch during the hot weather, like today, and by the kitchen stove during the long Oklahoma winters.

June 20, 1922: The cottonwoods along the Cimarron River near the ranch are thick and green with early summer, and every evening they are filled with birds. Just before suppertime, Gramma and I sit together snapping beans. We can hear the whistle of the train coming into Waynoka, six miles north of the farm.

Father and his horse, Sandy, returned to the farm by sundown. Although father gave up most of the animals and only plants a few fields with wheat and alfalfa since he began delivery work in town, there are still chores every evening. I brush and feed Sandy and the workhorse, Tess, and I feed the cows and chickens.

Tonight father told me he met a man off the train from Chicago who was selling silk he bought in San Francisco this past winter. After father took him to the local mercantile and then to a dressmaker who sews for the wealthy women in town, the salesman told father to choose several lengths of the silk in exchange for his services. Silk! All the way from China! Gramma and I opened the precious package in the kitchen and could hardly touch the fine cocoa charmeuse! What will we make with it? Gramma says we will have to give it some thought: it must be something special.

June 29, 1922: Today I went into Waynoka with Gramma. She met a friend at the mercantile, and they went off to talk while I went over to the Harvey House. My friend, Chris Schurig, whose father, Herman, is the Harvey House chef, and I had ice cream at the lunch counter. Chris and I are the same age and have been friends since he and his parents arrived in Waynoka four years ago. The Schurigs came from Germany to America just so Mr. Schurig could work for the Harvey Company as a chef. Chris went to school with me and now speaks very good English. We have a grand time at the Harvey House, especially since his father is always giving us leftover desserts and fresh bread and ice cream from the cooler when the lunchroom is empty! The Harvey Girls in their crisp black and white uniforms tease Chris like he is their brother.

Chris is learning to become a chef under his father's guidance. Today Chris asked me what I was going to do, now that I have finished school. Get married? He winked at me mischievously. Who would I marry out here in Woods County? A cowboy, he said, or one of the railroaders always giving me a nod? I'm not going to marry a railroader or a cowboy, I told Chris. He laughed and said I was going to have to go a long way from Waynoka to find someone who was not working on a horse or along the railroad.

Tonight I sat in my room looking out my window at dusk falling into the cottonwoods that follow the Cimarron River. Across the valley the railroad tracks cut southwest to Canadian, Texas, and then to Amarillo, and from Amarillo the Santa Fe tracks cross Texas into New Mexico, New Mexico into Arizona, and then all the way across the desert to California. People who come into the Harvey House know all those places. But they are so far away! How would a farm girl ever get there? I could never leave father and Gramma. Maybe I'll marry a cowboy after all?

July 5, 1922: Today I put on one of those crisp black and white Harvey Girl uniforms and became a Harvey Girl for just four hours! Gramma and father and I were in town for the afternoon when a rider came galloping on horseback into the depot area, shouting that there had been an accident south of town. The supper train had just departed Waynoka for Amarillo. After crossing the Cimarron River, out on the flats, it struck a huge old cow that had wandered onto the tracks. With the sun directly in his eyes, the engineer had not seen the animal until it was too late to stop the train. The train struck the cow broadside and was derailed. What a terrible accident! The engineer was killed! And several passengers and one of the brakemen were seriously injured.

Of course, father and Sandy headed directly out to the train wreck with several other local men and their wagons. I went into the lunchroom where Mr. Schurig and the manager were organizing the Harvey employees for the passengers, who would be returning to town by wagon in the next few hours. Waynoka has only a small boarding house across the street from the depot. Mrs. Bright, who owns the largest house in downtown Waynoka, said she could put five or six of the passengers up for the night and would organize her neighbors to do the same.

Chris Schurig came into the lunchroom and told Mr. Teafly, the Harvey House manager, that several of the Harvey Girls who had the afternoon off had left town and gone on a picnic somewhere along the river. They would never be found in time. Mr. Teafly, looking flustered and harried, turned to Gramma and me: "Marianne Brown," he said, "I've known you for almost three years. I think you would make a very good Harvey Girl for a day. What do you say? There

are uniforms upstairs in the girls' dormitory. Henrietta can help you get dressed and show you a few things in the lunchroom before the passengers begin returning."

I was speechless! I wasn't sure I could be a Harvey Girl, even for a few hours! But Gramma smiled and took me by the arm. "She will make a marvelous Harvey Girl!" Gramma told Mr. Teafly. "Come on, I'll go upstairs with you and help you find a uniform."

And up we went. Henrietta pulled out a fresh uniform that belonged to her roommate, Sally, from Wichita. After I dressed hurriedly, Henrietta fastened the bow on my blouse and positioned Sally's Harvey Girl pin securely below it. Gramma was so excited I told her maybe she was the one who should be a Harvey Girl, even for just a day!

"Oh, yes!" said Gramma, "I would love to have been a Harvey Girl and seen the West by train!"

Henrietta and I joined three other Harvey Girls who were already preparing the tables for customers. They were making fresh coffee and putting out oven-hot pies and bowls of cool fruit for the returning passengers. Chris had donned a busboy's uniform and helped me set tables. Every fork and spoon, every napkin and salt shaker, had to be placed just so. Fortunately, Chris had been around the Harvey House long enough to know just what to do. We were both nervous, but didn't dare giggle or talk. Mr. Teafly looked as if he were about to have a fit of nerves as he ran from the kitchen to the lunchroom to the Santa Fe telegrapher and back again!

Gramma went over to Mrs. Bright's house to help her prepare for the overnight visitors. A train will be coming through Waynoka around midnight, and many of the stranded travelers will be able to take that train on to Amarillo if the tracks are cleared by that time. The poor engineer's family is in Kansas; his body will be shipped home tomorrow.

August 16, 1922: More than a month has passed since I became a Harvey Girl, yet I still get up in the morning surprised to find I am in my little room above the Santa Fe depot where all the Waynoka Harvey Girls live. Mr. Teafly was so impressed by my work that afternoon after the train wreck that he offered me a job the very next day! I was uncertain about moving out of father's house on the farm, but Gramma told me she would come in every day if I wanted and that I could come home on my day off. That first afternoon at the lunch counter was almost unmanageable, but even with the clamoring and nearly hysterical passengers, I found the work of a Harvey Girl to be challenging and even fun. I'd never spoken to so many people from so many places—Boston, Kansas City and St. Louis, Chicago, Philadelphia, and New York. There was even an Austrian prince with a bandaged eye who kissed my hand when I brought him a cup of coffee and a fresh piece of blueberry pie!

So, here I am, a Harvey Girl. I work the lunch counter. We serve three trains a day as well as the Santa Fe railroadmen who come and go at all hours, and of course, local folks come in for meals, too. I have made so many new friends—Sally and Lisa, Henrietta, Gloria and Pam, all of them from Kansas—and of course I see a good deal of Chris, who helped me through the first few days when I felt homesick for the farm, especially in the evenings.

My pay is very good: thirty dollars a month, plus room, board, and tips, and the house does all of my laundry. I am able to save most of what I make. Father said his business is doing well—I see him every day, of course; he always stops for a cup of coffee and pie at the lunch counter when I am working! And Gramma comes in several times a week. Last week she surprised me with a dress made from the cocoa-colored charmeuse. All of my friends ask me where I bought it so they might be able to order one like it. She loves the Harvey House and tells me to enjoy this time of hard work and interesting people. And I am!

November 8, 1922: A week ago, Chris Schurig left Waynoka with his parents, bound for Needles, California, where Mr. Schurig will be the head chef at the El Garces Hotel. It is not uncommon for Harvey people to come and go—my first roommate, Pamela, asked for a transfer last summer and is now working at Casa del Desierto, the Harvey House in Barstow, California. But when Chris and his parents climbed on the train last Sunday evening, I thought I would never feel happy again! Chris is well on his way to becoming a fine chef like his father and has been assisting him in the kitchen for more than a year. We spent many an afternoon together here at the Harvey House or at the cinema with other Harvey employees, and Chris often went out to the farm with me for picnics or just to help out with chores. I told Gramma yesterday that the lunch counter will hardly seem as cheerful without Chris's happy face beaming from the kitchen. She said there will be other friends, but that

I would probably always miss Chris. We agreed to keep in touch, although Chris said he doesn't write many letters.

When the westbound train comes through, I think about its passengers reaching Needles, the same people who have disembarked from the train on the Waynoka platform walking into the Needles lunchroom where Chris and his family are a few days hence.

April 22, 1923: Gramma was here in Waynoka today when Mr. Frank, the Harvey superintendent from Chicago, came in on the eastbound train. He chatted for a while with Gramma and Mr. Teafly about the Harvey Houses he had just visited in Texas, New Mexico, and Arizona. Gramma asked him so many questions you'd think she was about to become a world traveler! After Mr. Frank left to talk with our new head chef, Mr. Emile Hess, Gramma turned to me and said, "Why, Marianne, you never told me you could request a position at any Harvey House along the Santa Fe! Why haven't you asked for a transfer? Think of the places you could see? Albuquerque or Santa Fe! Winslow, Arizona, or even Needles where the Schurig family is! Why, you could go to the Grand Canyon!"

I told Gramma that was much too far away from the farm and from her and father! But tonight when I was in my room reading, I got to thinking about all those places I'd heard about from the passengers and other Harvey Girls. I am nineteen years old now and can't imagine not working as a Harvey Girl. But can I imagine working as a Harvey Girl someplace that is not home?

Amarillo, Texas

October 5, 1923: This is the first moment I have had since I arrived in Amarillo to write in my diary! I have been in this dusty, noisy, bustling cowtown for almost a month. At the end of August, Sally and Gloria, fellow Harvey Girls at Waynoka, told me there were openings in Amarillo and that they were requesting to transfer together. I decided to go with them. After a difficult farewell to father and to Gramma, we boarded the westbound train with our bags. I watched every mile pass under the train as we crossed out of Oklahoma—the first time in my life!! We traveled through the stark, red, hill country near Canadian, Texas, where they say rattlesnakes are as common as crows, and into the Texas cattle country of Amarillo, the Queen City of the Plains! Thousands of cows await shipping in the stockyards surrounding town, and between the heat and the dust and the cattle themselves, there are days when the sun is a hazy orb in the sky. Cowboys off the trail from southern Texas mill around the streets and come to the Harvey House still wearing their spurs and chaps and weathered hats. They are a tad wild after weeks in the saddle, and they tell us that we Harvey Girls are the prettiest things they've seen, real or imagined, since they don't know when!

November 21, 1923: Cold northers blow straight through Amarillo. I told Gramma about the biting wind and how homesick I was for Thanksgiving in Oklahoma—and her delicious cranberry sauce—and next thing I know, she and father had sent me a package with a jar of her special sauce and a wool coat he'd ordered from Franklin Simon in New York. I don't know which makes me feel warmer—the coat or the cranberry sauce!

December 14, 1923: I would make but one exception to my rule about never marrying a cowboy: Will Rogers! Mr. Rogers came into Amarillo today and spent most of the morning talking to the Harvey House people about his travels. He tells stories and does rope tricks out beside the depot for everyone who will crowd onto the small platform. I liked him immediately—he is so lively and friendly and pokes fun at himself and all cowboys! I served him his dinner tonight. He wanted ham and eggs, which the chef never serves for supper, except for Mr. Rogers! He asked me where I was from, and he knew all about Waynoka! He said he had crossed that country on his horse many a time when he was a younger man and had even camped out under the cottonwood trees along the Cimarron River. I told him about my father's farm, and my Grandparents first homestead years ago on the Cherokee Strip, and he said, "Young lady, you and your family are exactly what the West is about: hard work, ingenuity, and beauty!"

I am still blushing! I will never fall asleep!

May 11, 1924: Today Gramma and father arrived on the train for a visit! I was working in the dining room so we did not have much time to talk, but tomorrow I will show them around Amarillo. Gramma

looked so elegant in her traveling suit, her eyes sparkling with excitement that she was in Texas. She even thought the Texas cowboys smoking outside of the Harvey House were "marvelous chaps!"

There are several large stores here in Amarillo, and father wants to see them all. He is thinking about opening his own mercantile in downtown Waynoka and wants to see what is offered in the big city shops.

I haven't seen Father and Gramma since December when I went home for five days after Christmas. I have so much to show them—the movie shows, the large homes of the Santa Fe officials and wealthy ranchers, the shiny automobiles parked outside the Harvey House at Sunday noon when most of the town leaders bring their families for lunch. There is to be a large May dance this weekend out at the Circle Y Ranch. I will wear the Nile green dress I ordered from Sears. Father said he would take Gramma, who had brought a lovely beaded, black silk crepe that she, too, had ordered from the catalog. We should make quite an entrance—it is so good to have them here!

December 20, 1924: Christmas will seem very empty this year without Gramma. She died of heart complications three weeks ago. I have returned to Waynoka for at least two months to help father with the house and farm and to help myself face the loss of Gramma. It is bitter cold, and even bundled up, it is difficult to do chores without shivering. Father works all day at his store in Waynoka and is quiet in the evening. He did bring me some fancy figured silk crepe that he bought from a New York salesman he has become friends with this past year—he sensed I needed something to fill my evenings. Gramma always said that melancholy feeds on idle hands, so despite my sadness, I've been making a Christmas dress. I can't imagine being festive this Christmas, yet sitting by the kitchen stove each evening this past month, I can just hear Gramma saying: "Marianne, Christmas is a time for joy!" I hadn't sewn anything since becoming a Harvey Girl, and I had a bit of trouble with the fine, slippery fabric. It will be a fine dress, but Gramma would have known how to do it better!

(continued on page 23)

Gramma's kitchen dress of lavender
cotton percale
1922

Marianne's cocoa silk charmeuse;
patent leather shoes
1922

Marianne's 1922 Harvey Girl uniform

Black felt hat

Copenhagen blue velvet hat

Marianne's top coat of tannish-gray wool
coating with opossum fur collar; silk lined
and warmly interlined
1923

Gramma's spring traveling suit of navy
blue wool serge with silk satin lining
1924

Chris's chef's uniform: white cotton,
reversible jacket and apron
1922

Nile green silk Canton crepe dress that
Marianne ordered from the Sears catalog
1924

Marianne's fancy figured silk crepe
with solid rust silk crepe trim
December 1924

Gramma's dress for the May Dance, black silk Canton crepe
with silk georgette crepe overlay and beaded trim
1924

Jim's felt western-style hat

Sand-colored hat

Johanna's felt hat with
Harvey Company emblem
brooch

Jim's Indian Detours driver uniform:
Cotton shirt, bandanna, and corduroy jodphurs
March 1926

Marianne's sand and brown
wool sweater with split skirt
for hiking and riding
1925

Johanna's courier uniform:
Navajo-style velveteen shirt and silver
and turquoise jewelry; split skirt and silk
scarf to protect against dust
1926

Chris's lightweight sport
crusher-style hat of wool felt

Johanna's black felt hat

Wool Shaker sweater coat and wool trousers
1926

Copenhagen blue sweater
and Oxford gray breeches
1926

Special New Mexico Harvey uniform for Indian
Ceremonial Days: Navajo velvet blouse, silver and
turquoise jewelry, and sateen skirt
1926

Jim's gray wool cap

Marianne's gray felt hat

Flannel shirt with wool trousers
1926

Gray suede cloth lumberjack blouse
with gray wool knickers
1926

Johanna's peacock wool worsted sweater coat with
light buff tuxedo front and matching blouse, skirt,
and hat; tan shoes
1926

Johanna's silk illusion veil with lace edge and beaded and embroidered lace bridal cap

Marianne's 1926 Harvey Girl uniform

Silk crepe dress with satin cummerbund
1927

Chris's navy blue wool worsted suit
1927

Marianne's bridesmaid dress of pink silk
crepe with satin cummerbund;
embroidered headband and trim on shoes
1927

Marianne's 1927 Harvey Girl uniform

Jim's gray wool worsted suit
1927

January 15, 1925: I received a letter today from Mr. King, the manager of the Amarillo Harvey House. He wrote to tell me that my position is still available, and that he hoped I would return to Amarillo soon. I miss my friends. I even miss the work in the dining room! I wrote Mr. King that I plan to return in early February.

Grand Canyon, Arizona

April 11, 1925: I was back at work in Amarillo about six weeks when a call came in from El Tovar, the grand Harvey Hotel on the rim of the Grand Canyon, asking our manager to send as many Harvey Girls as he could spare for the upcoming Easter Sunday sunrise service. Pam and Henrietta were the first to volunteer, and I was the third! We took the train from Amarillo yesterday and arrived in Williams, Arizona, this morning. A large touring car drove us up to the Grand Canyon where dozens of Harvey Girls from all over Arizona and New Mexico have gathered to help the El Tovar staff serve the hundreds of people who will come to the sunrise service on the Canyon rim tomorrow morning.

I had not been here thirty minutes when a man dressed in cook's white came running from the kitchen and threw his arms around me: it was Chris Schurig! He'd just been transferred to El Tovar as an assistant chef and had not even had time to write to me. Then and there I knew for certain I was going to enjoy my time here!

The Grand Canyon is larger and deeper and far more magnificent than any of the pictures or paintings can show! I will send Father a postcard and he still won't believe what I have to say about it!

May 18, 1925: With Pam, I permanently transferred to El Tovar and the Grand Canyon early this month. After returning to Amarillo, all I could think about was this gorgeous high desert sky and the beautiful colors of the canyon at sunset. Gramma would have loved this place! I'm hoping Father can come to visit soon, but he writes that he has begun calling on Dorothy Pringle, our neighbor whose husband, Victor, died three years ago.

El Tovar Hotel is perched on the very edge of the canyon wall. It is four stories high and was built of native boulders and huge Douglas fir logs brought all the way from Oregon. I have never seen such a fine place! In addition to the dining room and at least one hundred guest rooms, there are gardens and porches, art galleries and lounges, a music room, solarium,

even a garden on the roof! People come here from all over the world—you can hear almost any language you'd ever imagined. There are automobile tours around the rim of the canyon and mule trips down steep paths to the bottom. Across from El Tovar is Hopi House, where the Hopi Indians dance in the evening. Everyone who works here—Harvey employees, Santa Fe railroad people, plus tourist guides and traders—lives in the Grand Canyon Village. The Harvey employees have their own dormitories separated from the hotel, and here, unlike Waynoka or Amarillo, we are allowed to socialize with one another.

June 22, 1925: Today was my day off from the El Tovar dining room. With Pam and Chris, I descended the canyon on a mule! I was so terrified of some of the turns—the path was so narrow that the deep canyon dropped away thousands of feet just a few inches from the mule's hooves—I kept my eyes closed at times! I was grateful for my split skirt and the boots and hat I bought down in Flagstaff. El Tovar keeps split skirts like mine on hand for the use of women guests who arrive at the canyon ill-equipped to hike or ride horses. Chris loves the desert and has made the descent several times before. Why, with his tanned face under his western hat, you would never imagine he was once a shy German boy who struggled to speak English in Waynoka, Oklahoma.

We had our picnic lunch at the bottom of the canyon. I lay in the cool shade alongside Phantom Creek and thought of Gramma and how she would have loved this adventure from the top of the world to the bottom in one day—on a mule!

March 9, 1926: The Harvey Company and the Santa Fe Railway have begun a new car touring enterprise, called Southwestern Indian Detours. They will provide car tours of various natural wonders and sites in New Mexico and Arizona. Each car is to be driven by a professional driver and hosted by a woman courier who serves as guide. Today, several of the drivers and couriers came into the El Tovar dining room for lunch. The drivers wear tall boots and jodhpurs, crisp cotton shirts with neat bandannas, and a western hat. They are very handsome men and, I am told, the best drivers in the West. The women couriers wear split skirts with velvet Indian-style shirts. They have fine silver concho belts and a company hat. All of the couriers are college graduates, and these women know *everything* about Southwestern culture, geography, and history. I was a bit intimidated by them until one, Johanna Becker, asked me where I was from. I told her Waynoka, Oklahoma. She said she had been raised in Albuquerque, where she attended the university, but that she was born in Germany. I told her about Chris Schurig and his family, and before Johanna left, she said she hoped to see me again and perhaps meet Chris. "I need to practice my German," she said, laughing.

June 15, 1926: Johanna was at El Tovar briefly today, en route with a Harveycar of "dudes," as she calls them, to the Painted Desert. Chris was in the kitchen and I brought him out to meet Johanna after the lunch rush was over. They seemed to like each other immediately and were soon conversing in German about I don't know what, but they laughed a great deal. Johanna's driver, Jim Reid, came to tell her it was about time to round up the dudes. He tipped his hat to me and said he thought Harvey Girls were one of the true blessings of his job, which entailed hours of driving over terrible roads. I blushed like a schoolgirl. After Johanna and Jim had departed the hotel with their passengers, I wondered if all of the drivers were as friendly and handsome as James Reid.

July 18, 1926: Johanna and Jim travel all over New Mexico and Arizona and are regular visitors to El Tovar. I find myself checking the schedule each week to see what day their Harveycar will visit the canyon. Chris Schurig is always asking when I will see Johanna next. Last week when Johanna and Jim were here, they suggested we try to arrange a day off together so that we can all go out hiking and picnicking.

July 31, 1926: Midsummer: the Canyon is crowded with visitors. The wonders of the Grand Canyon and the Southwest attract people from all over the world—kings and queens, diplomats and generals, famous artists and writers, and movie stars. They ask me if I feel as if I am living in another world. Yes, I tell them. It *is* another world!

Chris and I sat looking out at the colors of the sky and the layers of the canyon at sunset last night, and we agreed that it is a view we will never become tired of!

August 26, 1926: I was invited to spend a few days during the Indian Ceremonials working at El Navajo, the Harvey Hotel in Gallup, New Mexico. El Navajo opened in 1923 and is decorated with wonderful Navajo rugs and sand paintings. The hotel is full, as is the entire town of Gallup, of visitors who have come to watch Indian dancers from all over the Southwest. The dancing begins at dawn and often continues all day into the evening. I slip out of the hotel between meal shifts to watch the dancers and to view a parade or walk along the crowded streets near the railroad tracks.

Instead of our traditional black and white uniforms, the Harvey Girls wear colorful gathered skirts, velvet Navajo blouses, and silver and turquoise jewelry during the Indian Ceremonials. It is a marvelous change from our usual garb, and the customers often ask us where they can buy the same skirt and blouse.

Jim and Johanna stopped in at El Navajo before embarking on a tour of the Painted Desert. Jim said I looked "splendid" in my ceremonial uniform. Johanna said "What he's trying to say is that you look beautiful, Marianne!"

I look forward to returning to my beloved Grand Canyon, but I shall miss wearing this elegant Southwestern outfit!

September 24, 1926: Today Jim, Chris, Johanna, and I went for an automobile tour on the Hermit Rim Road that follows the edge of the canyon west of Bright Angel Camp. One of Jim's friends, a Santa Fe executive, arranged for Jim to borrow a company Packard. He and Johanna arrived at El Tovar early morning. Chris and I packed a fabulous lunch of leftovers from the El Tovar kitchen, and we all departed from the Grand Canyon Village before nine o'clock.

I sat in the front seat with Jim while he skillfully drove the narrow dirt road that hugs the south rim. Jim is not allowed to talk while on duty driving the Harveycars, and Johanna kidded him about learning to converse with his friends while driving! After a while, Johanna and Chris, in the back seat, began to converse in German. They laughed so much that soon Jim and I were laughing, even though we had not the slightest idea what they were talking about! It didn't matter. I was so happy out there in that hot country beside Jim I could not have stopped smiling anyway.

We stopped for lunch at Hermit's Rest, a rustic rest and refreshment terminal built of stone and timber on the edge of the canyon, where Harveycar passengers, and anyone else who has come this far, can find food and drink and a chair inside the cool building or on the porch with the marvelous view. We decided to hike out away from the rest area and chose a picnic spot in the shade on a narrow strip of rock overlooking the canyon.

Jim told me he was raised in North Carolina, but came to Taos, New Mexico, with an uncle, when he was a teenager with tuberculosis. After recovering, Jim never left the Southwest. His uncle owned a sawmill, and Jim began driving wagons, and then trucks, down the steep Rio Grande Canyon between Santa Fe and Taos. When he heard the Indian Detours were hiring drivers, he applied. He had to pass a very rigorous driving test and learn to speak Spanish like a native. Jim, Johanna said, can find the road home from the middle of nowhere, fix a flat in pouring rain, and safely navigate the most precipitous mountain passes in the Southwest. "Some of the places he has to drive across I would not think of walking!" Johanna said. "Jim is the best. The best of the best!"

Jim asked me about my childhood in Waynoka. I told him about my grandmother and our farm and about my father, whose mercantile business was now the largest store in Woods County, Oklahoma. Jim chuckled and I blushed with embarrassment. But then Jim touched my hand and said his own father was a farmer and that he still missed the smell of the North Carolina fields after a good rain.

We arrived back at the Grand Canyon Village before supper. After freshening up, Johanna emerged looking terribly smart in a peacock and tan sweater outfit. Then she and Jim said farewell and drove down to Williams, where they will pick up their next group of dudes tomorrow morning. Jim squeezed my hand before leaving and said he hoped we could do this again very soon.

Chris and I sat on the steps of my dormitory and listened to the drums and singing from the Hopi House dancers after dark. Neither of us had much to say. But I knew Chris was thinking just what I was thinking: that Williams, Winslow, Gallup, all the vast Indian country where Jim and Johanna travel, are a very long ways away when you're falling in love with someone who is out there.

October 1, 1926: Today Jim and Johanna's Harveycar arrived unannounced at the Canyon, having had engine trouble out on the desert to the east, and the Grand Canyon Village was the closest garage with a good mechanic. A large crowd was in the dining room, and I could not even say hello to Jim. I was so flustered by his appearance at one of my tables that I bumped into Marcie, another Harvey Girl, and caused her to drop a tray of glasses. The commotion was awful! I apologized to Marcie about one hundred times. In tears, I fled into the kitchen where Chris asked me why I was so befuddled. I told him Jim and Johanna's car had broken down, and I had made a fool of myself in the dining room. Chris laughed and said I had been a Harvey Girl for too long: if things were not done according to the system, I just fell apart. I knew Chris meant to make me feel better, but I think maybe he's right!

Waynoka, Oklahoma

January 27, 1927: I came home to Waynoka just before Christmas . . . Father and Dorothy married on the twenty-seventh. Father seems ten years younger—perhaps it is the smile on his face and the sparkle in his eye when he is with Dorothy?!

Dorothy asked me if there was a young man out there in the desert whom I was missing. A cowboy? A railroader? I thought how Chris and I had joked all those years ago about how far I would have to go to *not* marry a cowboy or railroader! I miss Jim terribly—he went home to North Carolina for part of the winter. He writes me lovely letters every week. Johanna is in Albuquerque. Chris is still back in Arizona. I look forward to the time when we will all be in the same state again!

Grand Canyon, Arizona

April 4, 1927: I returned to El Tovar in February. Chris is here, but he will leave soon for Albuquerque. He and Johanna are getting married, and there are jobs for both of them at the Alvarado, so they will move there. How will I get along without them?! Jim now works with another courier, Margaret. He said he misses Johanna's jokes and feistiness. So do I.

May 7, 1927: Judith, our head waitress in the El Tovar dining room, fell ill with chicken pox, of all things, yesterday afternoon. There is a special tour group of businessmen from England at the Grand Canyon this entire week, and our manager, Mr. Bennett, decided that we must have a head waitress, period! Late last night he sent me to Judith's room for her uniform, and this morning I became the most reluctant head waitress in the Harvey system! I always knew Judith worked harder than anyone, overseeing all of the girls, the table settings, the dishes, and the trays, and the customers, too. But when she is up and around again, maybe by late next week, I will never again let anyone complain about how she has her own apartment and special privileges: a head waitress needs twice the energy and carries thrice the responsibility of any Harvey Girl!

July 10, 1927: I am on the train between Williams and Albuquerque: the hot brown and red desert speeds by my window. I am going to the Alvarado in Albuquerque for Chris and Johanna's wedding in which I will be maid of honor and Jim will be best man. Jim will meet me there—he has a tour of Canyon de Chelly and Chaco Canyon today and tomorrow and then will drive straight to Albuquerque after the dudes board the train at Gallup.

Alvarado Hotel, Albuquerque, New Mexico

July 14, 1927: The wedding was beautiful! It was held in one of the gardens at the Alvarado, where Chris's father is head chef. It was wonderful to be with Chris's parents again—they are like family to me. Johanna looked beautiful in her stylishly short wedding dress and flowing floorlength veil. I had never before seen Chris and Jim in suits, and I must say they looked impressive. I enjoyed wearing my pink silk bridesmaid's dress, styled like the bride's dress.

A photographer took dozens of photographs, but I could never forget this day, anyway. Jim asked me where *we* should get married—our families being so many miles apart in Oklahoma and North Carolina. I was speechless.

"We are getting married, Marianne, aren't we?" Jim asked me when I did not answer.

"Evidently," I said finally.

Jim chuckled. "I guess I should ask you first."

"Yes," I said. But before he could say anything more, I said, "I imagine the answer will be yes!"

Grand Canyon, Arizona

October 15, 1927: Tomorrow I will marry Jim Reid! Father and Dorothy; Jim's parents, Ruth and John Reid; and Johanna and Chris are guests at El Tovar tonight. We will marry in the El Tovar rooftop garden at ten in the morning. As we did for them, Johanna and Chris will stand up for us.

For our honeymoon, Jim and I will drive into Indian Country. Jim wants me to see the places he has told me about for the last year—trading posts, Navajo sheep camps, Hopi mesatop villages, and natural wonders like Monument Valley and Rainbow Bridge. We will be gone for several weeks.

Jim is thinking about opening his own trading post/tourist stopover on the Navajo Reservation. He has many friends out there, and after two years on the road, he wants to settle down in one place! Jim will still guide people privately around the desert, but he wants to be his own boss. I am a little nervous about living on a reservation. But I told Jim I am ready for the next adventure of my life—of *our* life! After all, I never thought I could be happy this far from Woods County, Oklahoma! Besides, Gramma and Grampa began their lives in the wild country of Oklahoma Indian Territory. During our honeymoon, we will look for a suitable place to settle.

As I close this diary tonight, I see that one chapter in my life is ending: my years as a Harvey Girl. The next time I open this book, I will begin a new chapter, as the wife of a guide and Indian trader. Maybe as a mother one day soon, and then as a grandmother? I know Gramma is smiling!

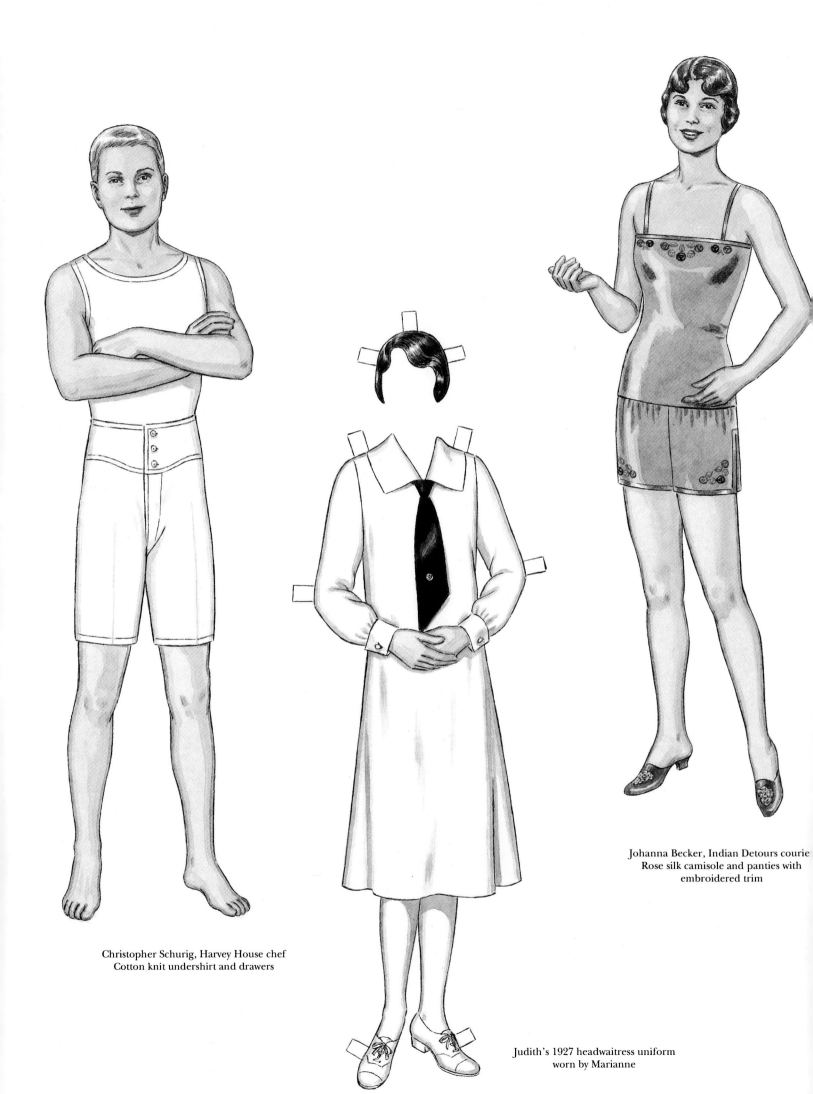

Christopher Schurig, Harvey House chef
Cotton knit undershirt and drawers

Judith's 1927 headwaitress uniform
worn by Marianne

Johanna Becker, Indian Detours courier
Rose silk camisole and panties with
embroidered trim